Why am I an insect?

Greg Pyers

www.raintreepublishers.co.uk
Visit our website to find out more information about **Raintree** books.

To order:
☎ Phone 44 (0) 1865 888112
🖹 Send a fax to 44 (0) 1865 314091
💻 Visit the Raintree Bookshop at **www.raintreepublishers.co.uk** to browse our catalogue and order online.

First published 2005 by Heinemann Library a division of Harcourt Education Australia, 18–22 Salmon Street, Port Melbourne Victoria 3207 Australia (a division of Reed International Books Australia Pty Ltd, ABN 70 001 002 357). Visit the Heinemann Library website at www.heinemannlibrary.com.au

Published in Great Britain in 2006 by Raintree, Halley Court, Jordan Hill, Oxford OX2 8EJ, part of Harcourt Education www.raintreepublishers.co.uk

A Reed Elsevier company

© Reed International Books Australia Pty Ltd 2005

09 08 07 06 05
10 9 8 7 6 5 4 3 2 1

Editorial: Helena Newton, Carmel Heron, Diyan Leake, Adam Miller
Design: Marta White
Photo research: Copperleife, Wendy Duncan
Production: Tracey Jarrett
Illustration: Richard Morden, Mordenart

Typeset in 21/30 pt Goudy Sans Book
Pre-press by Print + Publish, Port Melbourne
Printed and bound in China by South China Printing Company Ltd

The paper used to print this book comes from sustainable resources.

National Library of Australia Cataloguing-in-Publication data:

Pyers, Greg.
    Why am I an insect?

    Includes index.
    For middle primary school students.
    ISBN 1 74070 270 0.

    1. Amphibians – Juvenile literature.
    2. Dragonflies – Juvenile literature.
    3. Animals – Classification. I. Title. (Series: Classifying animals).
    (Series: Perspectives (Port Melbourne, Vic.)).

595.7

Acknowledgements
The publisher would like to thank the following for permission to reproduce copyright material: Bill Beatty: pp. **9**, **11**; FLPA/©Cisca Castelijns/Foto Natura: p. **6**; Richard Ford/Natural Visions: p. **24**; © Dwight Kuhn: p. **16**; Duncan McEwan/Naturepl.com: p. **22**; Photolibrary.com/OSF: pp. **4**, **12**, **15**, **19**, **26–7**, /AnimalsAnimals: p. **17**, /SPL: pp. **7**, **23**, /Peter Arnold: pp. **13**, **18**, **20–1**; WWI/Still Pictures/Andy Harmer: p. **14**, /Paul Hicks: p. **8**; © Duncan Usher/ Ardea London Ltd.: p. **25**.

Cover photograph of a dragonfly reproduced with permission of Photolibrary.com/AnimalsAnimals.

Every attempt has been made to trace and acknowledge copyright. Where an attempt has been unsuccessful, the publisher would be pleased to hear from the copyright owner so any omission or error can be rectified.

Contents

Words that are printed in bold, **like this**, are explained in the glossary on page 31.

All kinds of animals

There are millions of different kinds of animals. There are big animals and small animals. There are animals with bones and animals without bones. Some animals hatch from eggs and some do not. Some animals even look like plants!

But have you noticed that with all these differences, some animals are quite similar to one another?

Bees are small flying animals.

Sorting

We sort socks, T-shirts, and trousers into different drawers so that we can find the right clothes when we need them. Animals that are similar to one another can be sorted into groups. Sorting animals into different groups can help us learn about them. This sorting is called **classification**.

This chart shows one way that we can sort animals into groups. Vertebrates are animals with backbones. Invertebrates are animals without backbones. Insects are invertebrates.

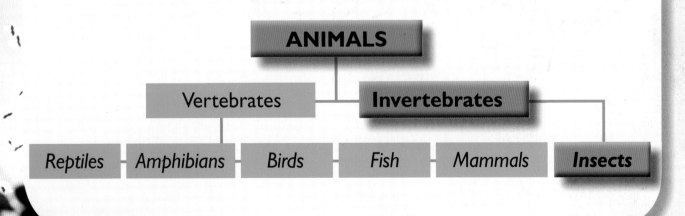

A dragonfly is an insect

Insects are one group of animals. They are a very large group of animals. Ants, moths, termites, and cicadas are insects. But why? What makes an insect an insect? In this book, we will look closely at one insect, the dragonfly, to find out.

As you read through this book, you will see a ✅ next to important information that tells you what makes an insect an insect.

FAST FACT

There are more than a million **species**, or kinds, of insects in the world. There are more insects than any other kind of animal.

A dragonfly is an insect with four wings.

Different dragonflies

There are more than 4000 species of dragonflies. The largest dragonfly species is 10 centimetres (4 inches) long and has a wingspan of 16 centimetres (6.3 inches). The smallest species has a wingspan of less than 2 centimetres (0.8 inch). A dragonfly does not have a sting, but it may bite if you pick it up.

Dragonfly habitat

Dragonflies' **habitats** are mainly near water. More dragonfly species are found in warm habitats than in cold habitats.

Compared to other kinds of insects, dragonflies are quite large.

A dragonfly's body

✔️ Like all insects, a dragonfly has a body with three main parts. These parts are the head, the **thorax**, and the **abdomen**.

Head

On its head a dragonfly has a mouth, two **antennae**, and two eyes.

Thorax

A dragonfly's thorax is in the middle of its body. The dragonfly's six legs and four wings are attached to the thorax. ✔️ All insects have six legs attached to the thorax.

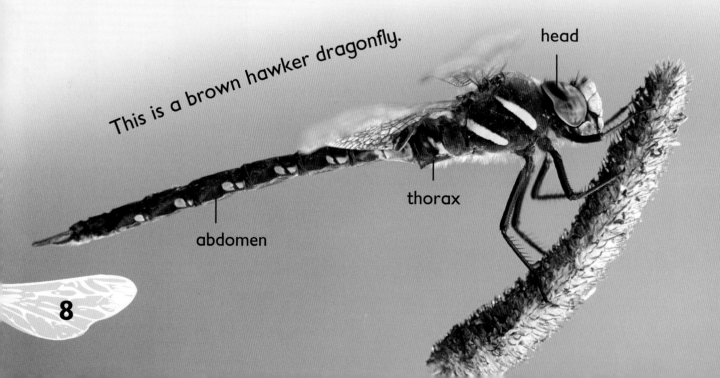

This is a brown hawker dragonfly.

head

thorax

abdomen

Abdomen

A dragonfly's abdomen is at the back end of its body. It is long and thin and bends easily. The abdomens of some insects, such as flies, are short and round.

Exoskeleton

✔ Like all insects, a dragonfly has no bones. Instead, it has an **exoskeleton**. The exoskeleton is like a hard skin, and it protects the dragonfly's body. The exoskeleton is also waterproof. It keeps water in and stops the dragonfly's body from drying out.

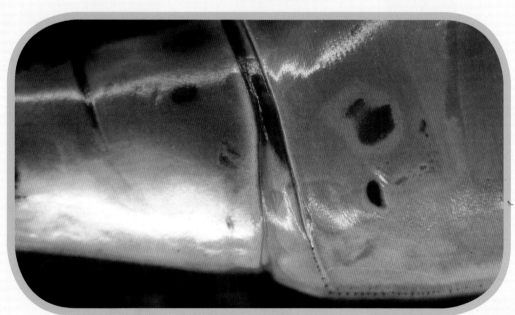

Many dragonflies have brightly coloured exoskeletons.

Inside a dragonfly

There are no bones inside a dragonfly. But there are **organs** that do important jobs. ✔ Like all insects, a dragonfly has a heart that is long and thin. It lies along the inside of the dragonfly's back. The heart pumps blood towards the dragonfly's head. The blood then flows back through the dragonfly's body.

FAST FACT

Bees have a honey stomach inside their **abdomens**. This is used for carrying **nectar** back to their hive. The nectar is made into honey and fed to the bee **larvae**.

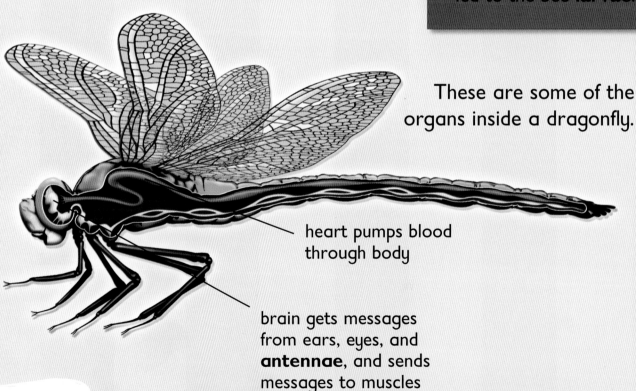

These are some of the organs inside a dragonfly.

heart pumps blood through body

brain gets messages from ears, eyes, and **antennae**, and sends messages to muscles

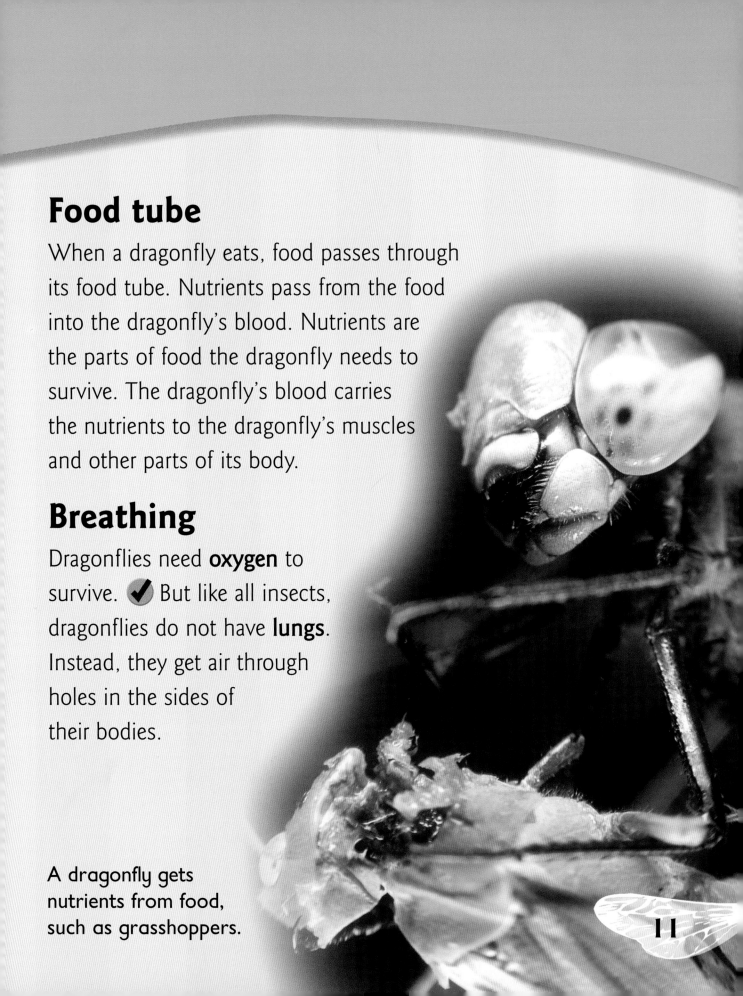

Food tube

When a dragonfly eats, food passes through its food tube. Nutrients pass from the food into the dragonfly's blood. Nutrients are the parts of food the dragonfly needs to survive. The dragonfly's blood carries the nutrients to the dragonfly's muscles and other parts of its body.

Breathing

Dragonflies need **oxygen** to survive. ✔ But like all insects, dragonflies do not have **lungs**. Instead, they get air through holes in the sides of their bodies.

A dragonfly gets nutrients from food, such as grasshoppers.

11

Senses

Like all insects, dragonflies have senses to help them find food and stay away from **predators**. Their senses also help them to find each other and to find their way around.

Eyes

Dragonflies have very large eyes. These give dragonflies excellent sight. ✓ Like all insects, dragonflies have **compound eyes**. Compound eyes are made up of hundreds of separate parts. Each part faces in a slightly different direction, giving a dragonfly an excellent all-round view.

A dragonfly's compound eyes wrap around its head.

compound eye

Antennae

A dragonfly has two very short **antennae** on its head. ✔️ All insects have antennae. Antennae are sense **organs**. They pick up smells from the air. Antennae can also sense whether the air is warm or cold.

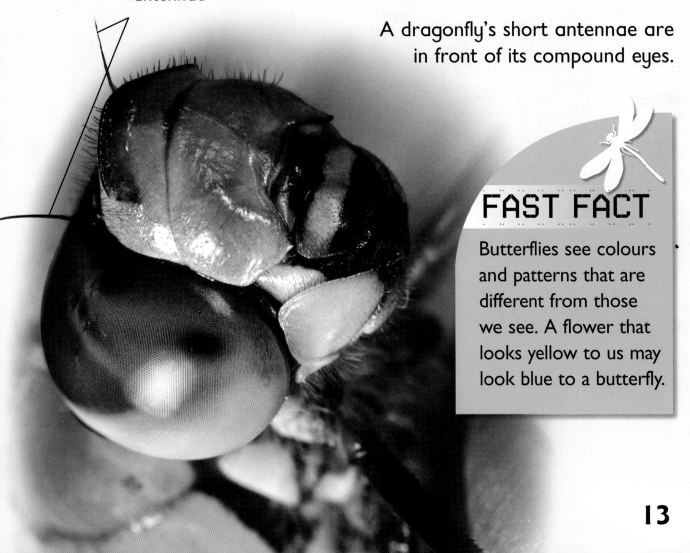

antennae

A dragonfly's short antennae are in front of its compound eyes.

FAST FACT

Butterflies see colours and patterns that are different from those we see. A flower that looks yellow to us may look blue to a butterfly.

Flying

Dragonflies are excellent fliers. Some dragonflies can fly as fast as 60 kilometres an hour (37 miles an hour). Dragonflies can stop and fly in one spot in mid-air. They can even fly backwards. Before it can fly, a dragonfly must warm up its body in the sun. ✔ All insects need the sun to warm their bodies.

A dragonfly can stop in mid-air while it looks for food.

Wings

A dragonfly's four wings are attached to its **thorax**. Strong muscles in the thorax make the wings beat up and down. When a dragonfly is flying, the front pair of wings go up as the back pair go down. A dragonfly beats its wings up and down around 30 times a second.

Most flying insects rest with their wings lying along their bodies. But when a dragonfly is not flying, its wings lie across its body.

A dragonfly's rear wings are almost as long as its front wings.

FAST FACT

Some insects, such as the head louse, do not have wings and cannot fly. The head louse moves from hair to hair by holding on with its claws.

Food

Dragonflies are **predators**. This means they kill and eat other animals. Most of a dragonfly's **prey** are other flying insects. These include flies and midges.

Finding prey

A dragonfly flies along the water's edge looking for prey. It may stop in mid-air, waiting for an insect to fly into view. With its large **compound eyes**, a dragonfly can see its prey very clearly.

A dragonfly can twist and turn in flight to catch other flying insects.

Catching prey

A dragonfly catches its prey in mid-air. It uses its legs to grasp its prey. It then begins to eat it while still flying. Sometimes, a dragonfly may have to land to eat. This happens when it catches a large insect, such as a cicada. A dragonfly's mouth has strong jaws. These can cut through an insect's **exoskeleton**.

Sometimes a dragonfly lands on a tree to eat a fly.

FAST FACT

Different insects have different types of mouths. A butterfly has a mouth like a straw, for drinking **nectar**. A cicada has a mouth that can stab into a plant to suck out the plant's juices.

Mating and laying eggs

Insects are a very large group of animals, and different insects have different life cycles. Male and female dragonflies **mate** when the weather is warm. The tip of a male's **abdomen** holds onto the female, just behind her head. When they separate, the female is ready to lay her eggs. But often, the male keeps holding on while she lays her eggs.

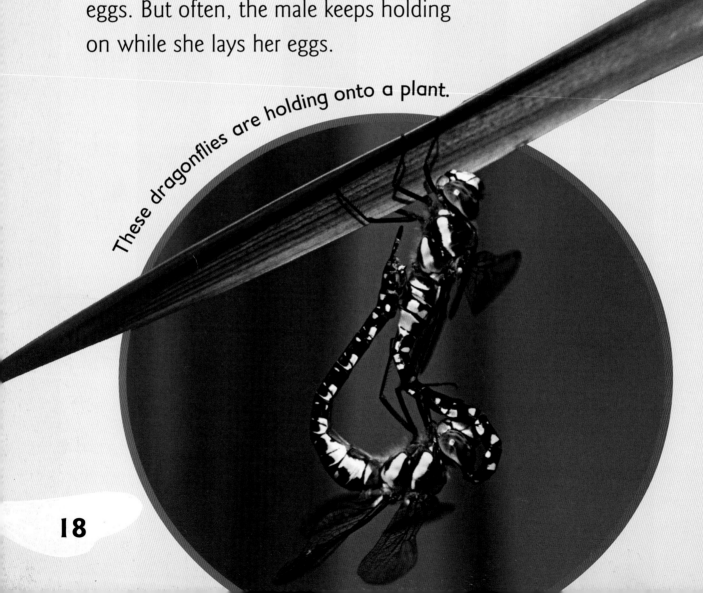

These dragonflies are holding onto a plant.

Laying eggs

The female flies over the water. She stops in mid-air and then pokes the tip of her abdomen below the water's surface to lay her eggs. There are some **species** of dragonflies that go right under the water to lay eggs. In many species, the male guards the female while she lays the eggs.

A female dragonfly may lay hundreds of eggs each year.

A female dragonfly may hold onto a water plant while laying her eggs.

Dragonfly larvae

In warm, **tropical** areas, dragonfly eggs hatch about 5 days after being laid. In cooler areas, the eggs may not hatch until the following summer. The animal that comes out of a dragonfly egg is called a dragonfly nymph or **larva**.

A dragonfly larva looks very different from an adult dragonfly.

Living in water

The dragonfly larva has no wings. It lives at the bottom of the pond, lake, or stream. It has large jaws and feeds on tadpoles and **aquatic insects**. It usually hunts by waiting for its **prey** to come close. Then it pounces. Dragonfly larvae do not need to come to the surface for air. They take in **oxygen** straight from the water.

Growing

As the dragonfly larva grows, it has to moult its **exoskeleton** ten or more times. Each time the larva moults, it has a slightly larger exoskeleton.

The dragonfly larva may leave its old exoskeleton on an underwater plant.

Becoming an adult

When a dragonfly **larva** reaches its full size, it is ready to become an **adult** dragonfly. Dragonfly larvae in the warmest parts of the world may be fully grown after just 60 days. In very cold places, dragonfly larvae may take 6 years before they are ready to become adults.

A dragonfly larva lives under water until it is fully grown.

FAST FACT

A moth is an insect. When its larva (a caterpillar) is fully grown, it spins itself a silk cocoon. Later, when the cocoon splits open, an adult moth comes out.

Coming out of the water

The dragonfly larva crawls out of the water. It may climb a tree trunk or a reed stem, or stay near the water's edge. The larvae of most **species** of dragonflies come out of the water at night. This is to keep out of sight of day-time **predators**, such as birds.

The larva stops moving now. Its **exoskeleton** begins to split. Slowly, the adult dragonfly comes out. In spring, if you look closely, you may see empty dragonfly exoskeletons on reeds and tree trunks.

It may take more than an hour for the adult dragonfly to climb out of the larva exoskeleton.

When the **adult** dragonfly first comes out, its wings are wrinkled and soft. This is because they have been squashed up inside the **larva exoskeleton**. The dragonfly pumps blood through veins in its wings and the wings begin to stretch into shape. The sun dries them and soon they become stiff. Then the dragonfly is able to fly.

A young dragonfly cannot fly until its wings have stretched and hardened.

24

Growing up

The young adult dragonfly flies away from water for a few days or weeks. During this time, it feeds on insects and its full adult colour develops. The dragonfly may then fly to a pond or stream many kilometres away. Some dragonflies stay at their home ponds. When the weather is warm, they will find a mate and the life cycle begins again. Adult dragonflies live for less than a year.

FAST FACT

Most insects live only for a few days, weeks, or months. A queen termite may live for 20 years.

An adult dragonfly stays the same size for the rest of its life.

Is it an insect?

A dragonfly is an insect because:

✓ it has an **exoskeleton** instead of bones

✓ it has a body made up of three main parts:
a head, **thorax**, and **abdomen**

✓ it has six legs

✓ it has a long, thin heart and no **lungs**

✓ it has **compound eyes** and **antennae**

✓ it needs the sun's warmth to heat up its body.

A dragonfly is an insect.

Test yourself: scorpions

There are more than 700 **species** of scorpions. Scorpions have a hard exoskeleton instead of bones. As they grow, scorpions shed their old exoskeleton. If a scorpion loses one of its eight legs, it grows a new one. Scorpions do not have antennae and their eyes are not compound eyes. A scorpion has a long tail with a sting on the end. This sting is used to kill **prey** and to protect itself against **predators**, such as meerkats.

Are scorpions insects? You decide. (You will find the answer at the bottom of page 30.)

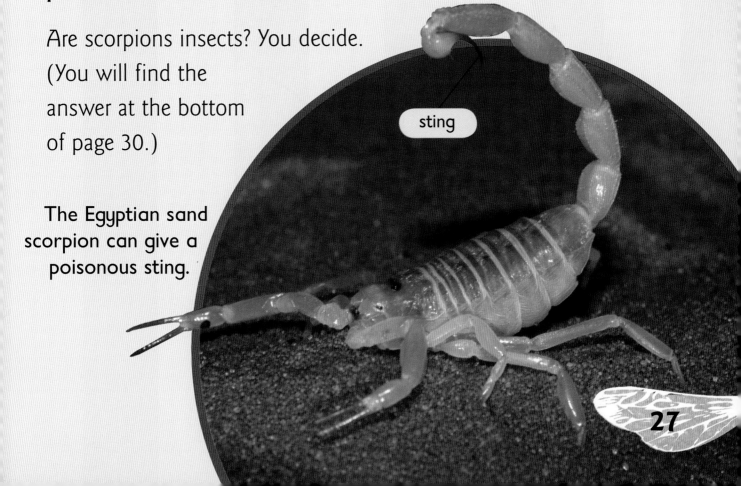

sting

The Egyptian sand scorpion can give a poisonous sting.

Animal groups

This table shows the main features of the animals in each animal group.

Mammals	Birds	Reptiles
backbone	backbone	backbone
skeleton inside body	skeleton inside body	skeleton inside body
most have four limbs	four limbs	most have four limbs
breathe air with **lungs**	breathe air with lungs	breathe air with lungs
most have hair or fur	all have feathers	all have scales
most born live; three **species** hatch from eggs; females' bodies make milk to feed young	all hatch from eggs with hard shells	many hatch from eggs with leathery shells; many born live
steady warm body **temperature**	steady warm body temperature	changing body temperature

Fish	Amphibians	Insects
backbone	backbone	no backbone
skeleton inside body	skeleton inside body	**exoskeleton** outside body
most have fins	most have four limbs	six legs
all have gills	gills during first stage; **adults** breathe air with lungs	breathe air but have no lungs
most have scales	no feathers, scales, or hair	many have some hair
most hatch from eggs; some born live	all hatch from eggs without shells	many hatch from eggs; many born live
changing body temperature	changing body temperature	changing body temperature

Find out for yourself

Next time you visit a pond or a stream on a warm day, look out for dragonflies. Watch how they fly. You may see how their back wings go up as their front wings go down. You may see dragonflies **mating** or a female laying eggs in the water.

For more information about dragonflies and other insects, you can read more books and look on the Internet.

Books to read

Go Facts: Insects, Paul McEvoy (A & C Black, 2003)

Minibeasts Up Close series, Greg Pyers and Robin Birch (Raintree, 2004 and 2005)

Variety of Life: Insects, Joy Richardson (Franklin Watts, 2003)

What's the Difference? Insects, Stephen Savage (Hodder Children's Books, 2002)

Using the Internet

You can explore the Internet to find out more about insects.
An adult can help you use a search engine. Type in a keyword such as "insects", or the name of a particular insect species.

Answer to "Test yourself" question:
A scorpion is not an insect. It belongs to a group of animals called arachnids. Spiders also belong to this group.

Glossary

abdomen back part of an insect's body

adult grown-up

antenna (plural: antennae) feeler on an insect's head, used for sensing

aquatic insects insects that live in water

classification sorting things into groups

compound eye eye made up of many separate parts

exoskeleton hard skin of an insect

habitat place where an animal lives

larva (plural: larvae) first stage in the life of some insects. For example, a caterpillar is a butterfly larva.

lungs organs that take in air

mate come together to make new animals

moult shed old skin

nectar sweet liquid made by flowers

organ part of an animal's body that has a certain task or tasks

oxygen gas that living things need to survive

predator animal that kills and eats other animals

prey animals that are eaten by other animals

species kind of animal

temperature how warm or cold something is

thorax middle part of an insect's body

tropical relating to areas in the world that are warm all year round

Index

Titles in the **Classifying Animals** series are:

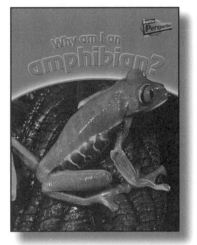

ISBN   1 74070 271 9

ISBN   1 74070 273 5

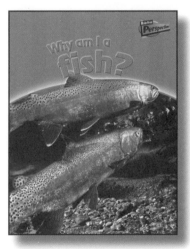

ISBN   1 74070 268 9

ISBN   1 74070 270 0

ISBN   1 74070 269 7

ISBN   1 74070 272 7

Find out about the other titles in this series on our website www.raintreepublishers.co.uk